Woza Albert!

PERCY MTWA was born and bred in Wattville, Benoni. From his youth he danced and played music in nightclubs in and around Daveyton. After leaving school he joined Dunlop Industries as a stores clerk and continued to dance and sing with his own group. 'Percy and the Maestros'. In 1979 director Gibson Kente gave him a role as singer/dancer in *Mama and the Load*, which played at the Market and Baxter Theatres and toured South Africa. It was during this time he met Mbongeni Ngema and the beginnings of *Woza Albert!* were conceived.

MBONGENI NGEMA was born in Umkumbane, Durban. He was first employed in Richards Bay as a hand-boy. This was followed by work with various companies for maximum periods of three months. He became a guitarist backing many plays in Durban including Lucky Mavundla's *Isigcino*, where he made his debut as an actor. He wrote and presented a play, *Too Harsh*, appeared in Kessie Govender's *Working Class Hero*, then wrote and, with Kessie's help, directed *The Last Generation*. In 1979 he came to Johannesburg and approached Gibson Kente for work, finally getting a character role in *Mama and the Load*, where he met Percy Mtwa.

BARNEY SIMON, Artistic Director of the Market Theatre, was born in Johannesburg. After backstaging for Joan Littlewood in the late 1950s, he joined Athol Fugard in Johannesburg's Dorkay House Rehearsal Room where *The Blood Knot* was first staged. He directed Fugard in *Krapp's Last Tape* and the first production of Fugard's own *Hello and Goodbye*. In 1974 he founded the Company with Mannie Manim, which made its home in Johannesburg's old Market in 1976. His other productions include *The Marat/Sade, The Seagull, The Maids, Happy Days, Woyzeck, Oedipus, The Crucible, Lysistrata, Mother Courage, Medea, Antigone, Death of Bessie Smith*, and *The Trojan Women*. His own plays include *Phiri* (a black musical version of *Volpone*), *Cold Stone Jug, Joburg Sis*, and *Miss South Africa* (6), seen at the National Theatre, London, with Yvonne Bryceland. Texts created with actors include *People, Storytime, Call Me Woman, Cincinatti*, and *Woza Albert!* Barney Simon is the three-time winner of the Breytenbach Epathlon for best director.

THE MARKET THEATRE COMPANY

The Market Theatre Company is the resident producing body at Johannesburg's Market Theatre. It was formed in 1974 by Barney Simon (Artistic Director) and Mannie Manim (Administrative Director) and a small group of actors. In 1975 it was awarded the tender to convert the old Johannesburg market building into an arts complex. The Company is totally without subsidy and exists solely from its box office. Its policy is to encourage the work of South African writers, directors and actors and to combine this with the staging of the best imported hits and great classical works and to make these available to all the people of South Africa. Also in 1975 the Market Theatre Foundation was formed. Its objects are to raise funds for the conversion and maintenance of the building and to administer the complex. This complex, unique in South Africa, now houses three theatres, an art and photo gallery, bookshop, bar and restaurant. The Foundation gratefully acknowledges the support from all economic levels of the public at large.

Information about the Market Theatre Company is available from P.O. Box 8656, Johannesburg, 2000, Republic of South Africa.

Percy Mtwa
Mbongeni Ngema
Barney Simon

WOZA ALBERT!

With production photos by Chris Harris and David Liddle

METHUEN DRAMA

Methuen Modern Play

Woza Albert! first published in Great Britain in 1983 as a
Methuen Paperback by Methuen London Ltd.

Reprinted in 1990 (twice) by Methuen Drama,
Michelin House, 81 Fulham Road, London SW3 6RB
Reprinted 1992

Set in IBM 10pt Journal by 🅰 Tek-Art, Croydon, Surrey
Printed and bound in Great Britain by
Cox & Wyman Ltd, Cardiff Road, Reading

ISBN 0 413 53000 0

*The front cover shows Percy Mtwa and Mbongeni Ngema in the
opening jazz fugue, photographed at the Riverside Studios,
London, by Chris Harris.*

Introduction

Now, upon application for a permit, all theatres in South Africa can be multi-racial. These theatres are in the White cities. There are no theatres in the Black townships: performances happen in halls — churches, schools, community centres — sometimes in cavernous cinemas. There are minimal facilities — few lights, no fixed seats, no carpets. High-heels sound. Cold-drink cans roll. Babies cry. Friends call to each other. Drunks heckle. People come and go. Performers must fend for themselves — and they do — in the broad, loud, triumphantly energetic 'township' style.

Mbongeni Ngema and Percy Mtwa met on such a township tour of *Mama and the Load*, a Gibson Kente musical, Ngema as an actor, Mtwa as a singer and dancer. They both felt the need for further challenges, and in their questioning and reading came upon Grotowski's *Towards a Poor Theatre*, and Peter Brook's *The Empty Space*. They stopped drinking and smoking and exercised their bodies, their voices, their resonators. They decided to create a piece together and hunted for a subject. One night in their touring bus, they found it. There was a heated argument on the Second Coming. What would happen to Jesus if he came back — to South Africa!

They began to read the Bible and to improvise. Finally they left *Mama and the Load* to concentrate on their piece. They approached Barney Simon, Artistic Director of the Market Theatre to collaborate with them because of his extensive experience in Black and non-racial theatre and because of the work that he had done in the creation of texts with actors.

After six weeks of intensive collaboration with Simon — writing, improvising, scouring the Gospels and the streets of Soweto and Johannesburg — the structure, text and title of *Woza Albert!* were born.

Most of the South African government's policies are the result, they say, of their Christian Nationalist principles. *Woza Albert!* is our fantasy of a Second Coming to South Africa by Morena, the Saviour.

Percy Mtwa
Mbongeni Ngema
Barney Simon

Woza Albert! was created in collaboration by Percy Mtwa, Mbongeni Ngema and Barney Simon.

It was directed by Barney Simon and performed by Percy Mtwa and Mbongeni Ngema.

It was first performed at the Market Theatre, Johannesburg, in 1981.

It was subsequently performed at the Mark Taper Forum, Los Angeles (1982), the Berkeley Rep., Berkeley (1982), the Traverse Theatre, Edinburgh (August-September 1982), Riverside Studios, London (September-October 1982), the ACT Theatre, Seattle (1983) and the Annenberg Centre, Philadelphia (1983).

Photos on pp. 4, 9, 11, 15, 18, 24, 48 (above), 59, 72 (above & below) and 78 are by David Liddell at the Traverse Theatre, Edinburgh. All the rest are by Chris Harris at the Riverside Studios, London.

The stage is lit by the house-lights. The set consists of two up-ended tea-chests side by side about centre stage. Further upstage an old wooden plank, about ten feet long, is suspended horizontally on old ropes. From nails in the plank hang the ragged clothes that the actors will use for their transformations. The actors wear grey track-suit bottoms and running shoes. They are bare-chested. Around each actor's neck is a piece of elastic, tied to which is half a squash ball painted pink — a clown's nose, to be placed over his own nose when he plays a white man.

Scene One

The actors enter and take their positions quickly, simply. Mbongeni sits on the tea-chests at the point they meet in the middle. Percy squats between his legs. As they create their totem, the house-lights dim to blackout.

On the first note of their music, overhead lights come on, sculpting them. They become an instrumental jazz band, using only their bodies and their mouths — double bass, saxophone, flute, drums, bongos, trumpet etc. At the climax of their performance, they transform into audience, applauding wildly.

Percy stands, disappears behind the clothes rail. Mbongeni goes on applauding. Percy reappears wearing his pink nose and a policeman's cap. He is applauding patronisingly. Mbongeni stares at him, stops applauding.

PERCY. Hey! Beautiful audience, hey? Beautiful musician, né? Okay, now let us see how beautiful his pass-book is! (*To appalled Mbongeni:*) Your pass!

MBONGENI (*playing for time*): Excuse my boss, excuse? What?

PERCY (*smugly, to audience with his back to Mbongeni*): Okay, I'll start again. You know you're a black man, don't you?

MBONGENI. Yes, my boss.

PERCY. And you live here in South Africa?

The climax of the jazz fugue.

MBONGENI (*attempting to sidle off-stage behind Percy's back*): Yes, my boss.

PERCY. So you know that you must always carry your pass.

MBONGENI. Yes, my boss.

PERCY. Okay, now what happens if you don't have your pass?

MBONGENI. I go to jail, my boss.

PERCY. And what happens if your pass is not in order?

MBONGENI (*nearly off-stage*): I go to jail, my boss.

PERCY (*wheels on Mbongeni*): H-E-E-EY! Your pass!!!

MBONGENI (*effusively*): OOOOhhh, my pass, my constable! (*Moves to Percy, holding out his pass.*) Here's my pass my lieutenant.

PERCY. Okay, now let's have a look. (*Examines the pass.*) Where do you work?

MBONGENI. I work here, my Captain.

PERCY. You work here? If you worked here your passbook would be written 'Market Theatre, Johannesburg'. But look, it is written 'Kentucky Southern Fried'. Is this Kentucky Southern Fried? And look at the date. It tells me you haven't worked in four years. This is vagrancy, you're unemployed. (*To audience:*) Ja, this is what I call 'loafer-skap!'.

MBONGENI. No, my Colonel, I am a guitarist, I've been playing music for five years, my boss.

PERCY. Hey, you lie, you fuckin' entertainer!

MBONGENI. It's true, it's true, my boss.

PERCY. Can you show me where it is written 'musician'? Hey? Where's a guitar? Where's a guitar? Where's a guitar?

MBONGENI. Ag, nee — my Brigadier, I am self-employed!

PERCY. Self-employed? (*Chuckling collusively to audience:*) Hell, but these kaffirs can lie, hey?

MBONGENI. Maar, dis die waarheid, but it is true — my General!

PERCY. You know where you should be?

MBONGENI. No, my boss.

'Is this Kentucky Southern Fried?'

PERCY. You should be in prison!

MBONGENI. No, my boss.

PERCY. And when you come out of prison, do you know where you should go?

MBONGENI. No, my boss.

PERCY. Back to the bush with the baboons. That's where you belong! Kom hierso! Section 29. (*To audience, pleasantly*:) Do you know about Section 29? That's a nice little law specially made for loafers like him. And I've got a nice little place waiting for him in Modder-B Prison. Kom jong! (*Pulls Mbongeni by his track-suit.*)

MBONGENI (*aside*): Shit!

PERCY (*threatening*): What did you say? Wat het jy gesê?

MBONGENI. Nothing — my President!

The policeman (Percy) chases the musician (Mbongeni) behind the clothes-rail.

Scene Two

Enter both actors with prison blankets wrapped around their shoulders. Both are singing a prison song, a prisoner's fantasy of his woman's longing for him:

SONG. Ha-ja-ka-rumba
    Ha-ja-karumba
    (*Solo*).   Bath'uyeza — uyez'uyezana?
               Bath'uyeza — uyez'uyezana?
               Kuthima ngizule kodwa mangicabanga
               Yini s'thandwa sithando sami ye —

    (*Chorus*).   Hajakarumba — hajakarumba.
               Hajakarumba — hajakarumba.
               [They say he is coming. Is he really coming?
               I am mad when I think of it.
               Come back my love, oh my love.]

Under the song, Mbongeni gives orders:

MBONGENI. Modder-B Prison . . . prisoners — line up! Body Inspection. Hey wena cell number 16. Inspection cell number 16. Awusafuni na? Awusafunukuvula vula hey wena we-neloda.

The prisoners' 'Towsa' dance'.

Vul'inggwza sisone. [Hey you, cell number 16. Inspection cell number 16. Are you hiding anything? Don't you want to show what is hidden — come on you men — show me your arses!] Prisoners inspection!

BOTH (*doing 'Towsa' dance, revealing empty orifices and armpits*): Ready for body inspection, my Basie! Blankets clear, my Basie! No tobacco! No money! No watch! My Basie! Mouth clear! Ears clear! (*Open mouths wide:*) Hooo! Hooo! (*Pull ear-lobes:*) Haaa! Haaa! My Basie!

PERCY. Hands up!

BOTH (*raise arms*): Arms clear, my Basie! (*Raise legs:*) Everything clear, my Basie! Also arse, my Basie!

MBONGENI. Inspection! (*They pull down their trousers, display bare backsides.*) See nothing hidden, my Basie! Prisoners! Lights out! (*Lights dim.*)

BOTH (*lying on the floor covering themselves with blankets*): Goodnight, Basie, goodnight. Dankie Baba, dankie. Beautiful arse, my Baba. Nothing hidden, my Basie.

Lights dim on sleeping figures.

Scene Three

PERCY (*singing in his sleep*): Morena walks with me all the way / Watching over me all the day / When the night time comes he's there with me / Watching over, loving me.

MBONGENI (*restless, stirring from sleep*): Hey man uyangxola man — uyangxola man. [Hey man, you making noise man.]

The singing continues.

MBONGENI. Hey! Hey, hey! Stop singing your bloody hymns man, you're singing in your bladdy sleep again! Morena! Morena hoo-hoo, there's no Morena here!

PERCY (*dazed*): I'm sorry. (*Silence. He begins to hum again.*)

MBONGENI (*kicks Percy, who jumps up, is chased*): Hayi man — isejelela. [This is prison man.]

PERCY (*cowering*): Morena, the saviour, is watching over you too, my friend.

MBONGENI. Morena, the saviour, here in Modder-B Prison?
  BULLSHIT!

  Lights up bright. Work yard. Actors holding picks.

MBONGENI. Prisoners! Work yard!

BOTH (*working and singing a work-song*):
  Siboshiwe siboshel'wa mahala
  Wen'utha senzenjani
  Siboshiwe siboshel'wa mahala
  Wen'utha senzenjani
  [They arrested us for nothing
  So what can we do?]

  Mbongeni hurts his hand, nurses it.

MBONGENI. It's this bladdy hard labour!

PERCY (*attempting comfort*): Don't worry my friend. Morena
  is over there, he's watching over us.

MBONGENI. Morena. Here in prison?

PERCY. He's watching over you too.

MBONGENI (*kicking at him, chasing him*). Morena here??
  BULLSHIT!!

Scene Four

MBONGENI. Prisoners! Supper!

BOTH (*running*). Supper! Supper! Supper!

  *Transforms to supper-time. Prisoners racing around in a circle,
  carrying plates, handing them in for food. Mbongeni bullies
  Percy out of the way.*

PERCY. Thank you, soup, Baba. Thank you, Baba.

MBONGENI. Soup, Baba. Thank you soup, Baba, thank you
  Baba.

PERCY. Porridge, Baba. Little bit of sugar, Baba.

MBONGENI. Porridge, Baba! Porridge. A little bit of sugar,
  Baba. A little bit of sugar, Baba. Thank you, Baba.

PERCY. A little bit sugar, Baba. Please, little bit, Baba. Thank
  you, Baba. Thank you, Baba, too much sugar, Baba.

'A little bit sugar, Baba.'

MBONGENI. Sugar . . . (*Reaches for Percy's food. Percy points to a guard, stopping Mbongeni who smiles to the guard.*) No complaints, my boss. Geen klagte nie.

PERCY. No complaints, Baba.

Mbongeni eats in growing disgust; Percy with relish.

MBONGENI (*spits on the floor*): Ukudla kwemi godoyi lokhu [This is food for a dog] — No, a dog wouldn't even piss on this food. Ikhabishi, amazambane, ushukela, ipapa, utamatisi endishini eyodwa — ini leyo? [Cabbage, potatoes, sugar, porridge, tomatoes in one dish — what is this?]

PERCY (*eating unconcerned*): Thank you Morena for the food that you have given me. Amen.

MBONGENI (*turns on him, furious*): Hey uthini Amen? [What do you say Amen for?] — For this shit? Thank you Morena for this shit?

Percy crawls away. Mbongeni beckons him back.

MBONGENI. Woza la! [Come here!]

Percy hesitates.

MBONGENI (*moves threateningly; points to the ground at his feet*): Woza la!

Percy crawls over reluctantly.

MBONGENI. On your knees!

Percy, terrified, gets down on his knees.

MBONGENI. Pray! Mr Bullshit, I'm getting out of here tomorrow. Pray to your Morena, tell him thanks for me. I'll never listen to your voice again!

Mbongeni pushes Percy forward on to the floor. Percy goes down with a scream that becomes a siren.

Blackout.

Scene Five

The siren transforms into train sounds. Lights up. Both men are sitting back-to-back on boxes, rocking as in a train. Mbongeni

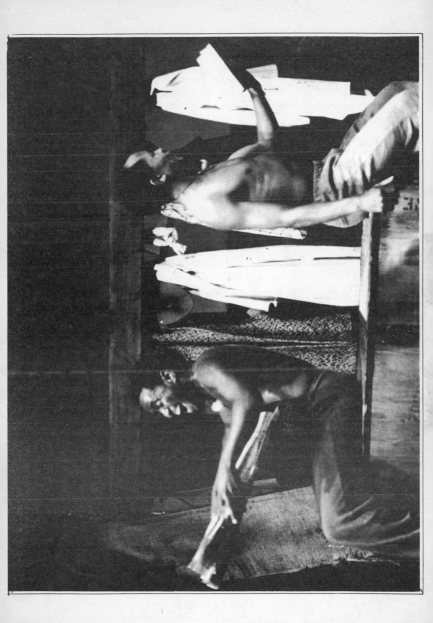

*is reading a newspaper, Percy a Bible. Mbongeni spits out of the
window, sits again.*

PERCY (*evangelically*): Blessed are those that are persecuted
for rightousness' sake, for theirs is the Kingdom of Heaven.
Blesséd are ye when men shall revile ye and persecute ye
and shall send all manner of evil against ye falsely, for thy
sake. Rejoice, and be exceedingly glad for great is the
reward of heaven. For so persecuted they —

MBONGENI (*turns on him, hits him on the head with newspaper*):
Hey! Persecuted? Prosecuted! Voetsak! Voetsak! (*Recognises
his former fellow prisoner*:) Hey, brother Bullshit! When did
you come out of prison? They promised me they would keep
you in for life!

PERCY. Be careful, my friend, of the anger in your heart. For
Morena will return and bear witness to our lives on earth and
there will be no place to hide. He will point his holy finger
and there will be those who rise to heaven and those who
burn in hell. Hallelujah! I hope you're not one of them!

MBONGENI. Rise to heaven? Where is heaven?

PERCY. It is the Kingdom of God.

MBONGENI. Up there? Neil Armstrong has been there.

PERCY. Neil Armstrong?

MBONGENI. Hallelujah! He's been right up to the moon and
he found a desert, no god!

PERCY. My brother, I don't care what you or your friend on the
moon say, because I know that he will return to his father's
kingdom on earth, even as I know that his father has heard
your blasphemies and forgiven you!

MBONGENI. Where does his father live? In Jerusalem?

PERCY. The Lord, our father, is everywhere.

MBONGENI. And Morena, the saviour, is coming to South
Africa?

PERCY. Hallelujah!

MBONGENI. How is he coming to South Africa? By South
African Airways jumbo jet? (*He transforms into a photographer
photographing the audience*.) And everybody will be waiting
in Johannesburg at Jan Smuts airport. Pressmen, radiomen,

South African television, international television, ABC, NBC, CBS, BBC, and they will all gather around — (*He turns to Percy, who has transformed into the Prime Minister with pink nose and spectacles.*) — our honourable Prime Minister!

Scene Six

PERCY (*moving forward ingratiatingly into spotlight*): Thank you very much, thank you very much. My people, Morena is back and South Africa has got him! I hope that the free world will sit up and notice whose bread is buttered and where! Let them keep their boycotts, their boxers, rugby players, and tennis racketeers. Stay home Larry Holmes! Stay home John McEnroe! We have got Morena! But there is already rumours going around that this is not the real Morena, but some cheap impostor. And to those that spread such vicious rumours I can only say, 'Tough luck friends! He chose us!' (*Raises his hands in V-signs, laughs.*)

Blackout.

Scene Seven

Lights up on Mbongeni wearing a Cuban army cap and smoking a fat cigar.

PERCY (*as announcer*): And now ladies and gentlemen, on the hotline straight from Havana — the comrade from Cuba — Fidel Castro! Sir, have you got any comment to make on the impending visit of Morena to South Africa?

MBONGENI (*laughing*): Morena in South Africa? Who's playing the part? Ronald Reagan?

Blackout.

The Prime Minister.

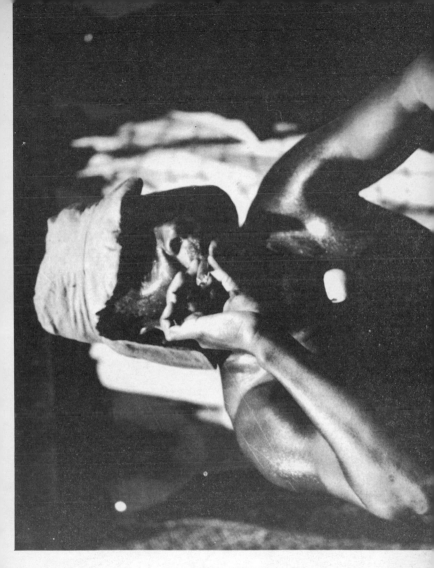

Fidel Castro.

Scene Eight

Lights up on Percy playing cool bongo on boxes.

MBONGENI (*dancing flashily*): And now for you to see on
Black TV — the face of Black South Africa! (*Enjoying the
bongo, dancing up to the player.*) Beautiful music my brother,
cool sound, man, cool! Real cool! Beautiful music, oh yeah,
oh yeah. Now tell me, my brother — what would you say —
if Morena — walks in — right through that door?

PERCY (*making a rude finger-sign*): Aay, fok off man!

Blackout.

Scene Nine

*Lights up bright on Percy, now a young street meat-vendor.
The boxes are his stall. His is swatting flies with a newspaper held
in one hand. His other hand holds a second newspaper as shade
against the sun.*

MBONGENI (*enters, singing, as a labourer-customer*):

(*Song*):   Siyitshil'igusha sayigqiba
Siyitshil'igusha sayigqiba
Muhla sitsh'igusha.
Wena wendoda wawuphina
Wena wendoda wawuphina
Muhla sitsh'igusha.
[We ate and finished a big sheep the other day.
Where were you when we blessed ourselves with a sheep?]

MBONGENI. Hullo, my boy.

PERCY. Hello, Baba.

MBONGENI (*not tempted by the display*): Ehhh, what meat
can you sell me today?

PERCY. I've got mutton, chicken, and nice sausages. (*Swats a
fly on the sausages.*)

MBONGENI. Oh yeah . . . the chicken does not smell nice, hey?
Must get some cover, some shade from the sun, hey?
(*Deliberating.*) Ehhh, how much are those chops?

The meat-vendor and his customer.

'Morena? Here in South Africa?'

PERCY. It's two rand fifty, Baba.

MBONGENI. Two rand fifty? Are they mutton chops?

PERCY. Ehhh, it's mutton.

MBONGENI. No pork?

PERCY. No pork, Baba. I don't like pork.

MBONGENI. Okay my boy, give me mutton chops. Two rand fifty, hey? Where's your mother, my boy?

PERCY. She's at work.

MBONGENI. She's at work? Tell her I said 'tooka-tooka' on her nose. (*Tickles the boy's nose.*) She must visit me at the men's hostel, okay? Dube hostel, room number 126, block 'B', okay? Bye-bye, my boy. 'B', don't forget. (*About to leave, he turns astonished at sight of — invisible — TV interviewer.*)

PERCY (*awed by TV-interviewer*): Hello, Skulu. I'm fine, thanks. And you? (*Listens.*) Morena? Here in South Africa? What shall I ask from Morena if he comes to South Africa? Baba, I want him to bring me good luck. So that the people that come will buy all this meat. And then? I want him to take me to school. Sub-A, uh huh. (*Watching the interviewer leave.*) Thank you, Baba. Inkos'ibusise [God bless]. Yeah, Baba . . . Au! TV!

Blackout.

Scene Ten

Lights up, dim, on Mbongeni as Auntie Dudu, an old woman, wearing a white dust-coat as a shawl. She is searching a garbage bin (upturned box). She eats some food, chases flies, then notices the interviewer. She speaks very shyly.

MBONGENI. Hey? My name is Auntie Dudu. No work my boy, I'm too old. Eh? (*Listens.*) If Morena comes to South Africa? That would be very good. Because everybody will be happy and there will be lots and lots of parties. And we'll find lots of food here — (*Indicates bin.*) — cabbages, tomatoes, chicken, hot-dogs, all the nice things white people eat. Huh? (*Receives tip.*) Oh, thank you, my boy. Thank

you, Baba. Inkos'ibusise. [God bless.] God bless you. Bye
bye, bye bye . . .

A fly buzzes close. She chases it.

Fade.

Scene Eleven

*Lights up bright on a barber's open-air stall. Percy — the
barber — is sitting on a box, Mbongeni — the customer —
between his knees. Auntie Dudu's shawl is now the barber's
sheet.*

PERCY. Ehh, French cut? German cut? Cheese cut?

MBONGENI. Cheese cut.

PERCY. Cheese cut — all off!

MBONGENI (*settling*): That's nice . . . How much is a cheese
cut?

PERCY. Seventy-five cents.

MBONGENI. Aaay! Last week my cousin was here and it was
fifty cents.

PERCY. Hey, you've got very big hair my friend. (*He begins
cutting hair.*)

MBONGENI (*squirming nervously during the — mimed —
clipping, relaxing at the end of a run*): That's nice. What
machine is this?

PERCY. Oh, it's number ten . . .

MBONGENI. Number ten? Ohhh.

PERCY. Though it's a very old clipper.

MBONGENI. That's nice. (*More cutting, more squirming.*) That's
nice. Where's your daughter now?

PERCY. Ohh, she's in university.

MBONGENI. University? That's nice. What standard is she
doing in university?

PERCY (*clipping*). Ohhh, she's doing LLLLLB. I don't know,
it's some very high standard.

The barber and his client.

MBONGENI. Oh yeah, LLB.

PERCY (*confirming with pleasure*): Uh huh, LLB.

MBONGENI. That's nice! I remember my school principal failed seven times LLB!

PERCY. Ohhh, I see! I understand it's a very high standard.

MBONGENI. Tell me my friend, but why don't you apply for a barbershop? Why do you work in the open air where everyone is looking?

PERCY (*continuing clipping*): Aaahh, don't ask me nonsense. I had a barbershop. But the police came with the bulldozers during the Soweto riots.

MBONGENI. Ooohh, 1976?

PERCY. Uh huh. During the times of black power. Everything was upside down . . . (*To the invisible interviewer as he enters:*) Oh, hello, Skulu. I'm fine, thanks. And you? (*Listens.*) Morena? Here, in South Africa?

MBONGENI. That's nice.

PERCY (*clipping, talking excitedly*): Well now, I want him to build me a barbershop in a very big shopping centre in Johannesburg city, with white tiles, mirrors all over the walls, and customers with big hair! (*The clipper gets caught in Mbongeni's hair. He struggles.*)

MBONGENI. EEEEceeeiiiiii!

Blackout.

Scene Twelve

Lights up. Percy and Mbongeni are coal-vendors, soot-stained sacks on their heads. They are climbing on to boxes — a coal lorry — taking off.

PERCY & MBONGENI. Hey! Firewood for sale! Coal for sale! Smokeless coal for sale! Firewood for sale! (*They make the sound of the lorry's engine revving. The lorry moves off.*)

PERCY. *Coal for sale!* Hey wena, Auntie Ma-Dlamini, phum'endlini. [Hey, you, Aunt Dlamini, come out of your house.] (*He spies a young girl, gestures.*) Dudlu — mayemaye,

The coal-vendors.

Threading the needle.

the sugar the pumpkin. [Hallo there, hi hi, you are the sugar, the pumpkin.]

MBONGENI. Red light! Hey wena! [Hey you!] Driver — awuboni irobbot? [Can't you see the red light?]

PERCY. Don't you see the red light?

MBONGENI. Awuboni la uyakhona? [Don't you see where you're going?]

PERCY. He hasn't got a licence.

Noise of the lorry revving. They discover the invisible interviewer below turn to him impatiently.

PERCY. What? Morena here in South Africa? You're talking rubbish! (*Lorry sounds again. It jerks forward.*) Smokeless coal for sale! Firewood for sale! (*Looks back.*) Putsho putshu ikaka kwedini. You're talking shit, boy.

MBONGENI. Inkanda leyo-kwedini-iyashisa he? [Your prick is hot, boy — heh?]

Percy looks back contemptuously and makes a rude sign with his finger as the lorry drives off.

Fade.

Scene Thirteen

Lights up on Mbongeni entering as a fragile, toothless old man. He sings throughout the following action. He settles on the boxes, attempts to thread a needle. His hands tremble but he perseveres. He succeeds on the third, laborious attempt and begins to sew a button on his coat.

MBONGENI (*humming*):
Bamga-lo-kandaba bayimpi
Heya we-bayimpi izwelonke
Ngonyama ye zizwe
Ohlab'izitha
UNdaba bamgwazizwe lonke okazulu
Amambuka nkosi

[The soldiers of our enemies have come to attack the king
They are coming from the four corners of the world to
    attack the Lion

We must kill the enemies
They are attacking him from all over the world, the son of
    Zulu
These strangers from another place attack our King.]

Mbongeni becomes aware of the (invisible) interviewer.
Laughs knowingly.

MBONGENI (*speaking*). Eh? What would happen to Morena if
he comes to South Africa? What would happen to Morena is
what happened to Piet Retief! Do you know Piet Retief? The
big leader of the white men long ago, the leader of the
Afrikaners! Ja! He visited Dingane, the great king of the
Zulus! When Piet Retief came to Dingane, Dingane was sitting
in his camp with all his men. And he thought, 'Hey, these
white men with their guns are wizards. They are dangerous!'
But he welcomed them with a big smile. He said, he said,
'Hello. Just leave your guns outside and come inside and eat
meat and drink beer.' Eeeeii! That is what will happen to
Morena today! The Prime Minister will say, just leave your
angels outside and the power of your father outside and
come inside and enjoy the fruits of apartheid. And then,
what will happen to Morena is what happened to Piet Retief
when he got inside. Dingane was sitting with all his men in his
camp, when Piet Retief came inside. All the Zulus were singing
and dancing . . . Bamya-lo-Kandaba payimpi . . . (*Repeats
snatches of the song.*) And all the time Dingane's men were
singing and dancing, (*Proudly*) they were waiting for the signal
from their king. And Dingane just stood up . . . He spit on
the ground. He hit his beshu and he shouted,
Bulalan'abathakathi . Kill the wizards! Kill the wizards! Kill
the wizards! And Dingane's men came with all their spears.
(*Mimes throat-slitting, throwing of bodies.*) Suka! That is
what will happen to Morena here in South Africa. Morena
here? (*Disgusted.*) Eeii! Suka!

Blackout.

Scene Fourteen

Lights flash on, Percy, an airport announcer, is standing on a box,
calling out.

PERCY. Attention, please! Attention, please! Now this is a great moment for South Africa! The Lord Morena has arrived! The jumbo jet from Jerusalem has landed! Now lay down your blankets, sing hosanna, hosanna, lay down your presents. Hey, you over there, move away from the tarmac! (*More urgently*.) Move away from the runway! Move away!

MBONGENI (*rushing in as a photographer*): Hosanna! Hosanna! Son of God! 'Hosanna nyana ka thixo!' ['Son of God'.] Hey, what will you say if Morena comes to you? (*To a member of the audience*:) Smile, smile! (*He turns to Percy then back to the camera crew.*) Sound! Rolling! Slate! Scene twenty seven, take one. And action . . .

Scene Fifteen

Percy, wearing his pink nose and flash sunglasses, alights from the plane (box).

MBONGENI (*approaching him with a mimed microphone*): Happy landings, sir.

PERCY (*flattered by this attention*): Oh, thank you. Thank you.

MBONGENI. Well sir, you've just landed from a jumbo jet!

PERCY. Eh, yes.

MBONGENI. Any comments, sir?

PERCY. I beg your pardon?

MBONGENI (*arch interviewer*): Would you not say that a jumbo jet is faster than a donkey, sir?

PERCY. Eh, yes.

MBONGENI. Aaahh. Now tell me, sir, where have you been all this time?

PERCY. Around and about.

MBONGENI. And how is it up there in the heavens?

PERCY. Oh, it's very cool.

MBONGENI. Cool! (*Laughs artificially loud.*) So, I'm to understand that you've been studying our slang, too!

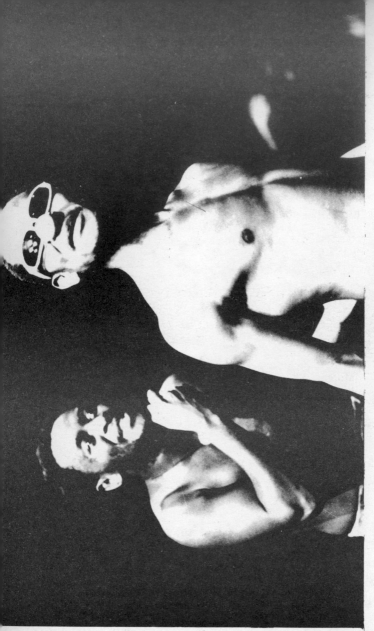

'How is it up there in the heavens?'

PERCY. Right on!

They laugh together.

MBONGENI. Now tell me, sir, in the face of all boycotting moves, why did you choose South Africa for your grand return?

PERCY. I beg your pardon?

MBONGENI. I mean, uuuh, why did you come here, sir?

PERCY. To visit my Great-aunt Matilda.

MBONGENI. Excuse me, sir?

PERCY. Yes?

MBONGENI. Your name, sir?

PERCY. Patrick Alexander Smith.

MBONGENI. You mean you're not Morena, sir?

PERCY. Who?

MBONGENI. Morena.

PERCY. Morena?

MBONGENI. Are you not Morena? (*To film-makers:*) Cut!!! Morena! Where is Morena? (*Percy minces off, insulted. Stage dim, Mbongeni wanders across stage, calling disconsolately.*) Morena! Morena! Morena! M-o-o-o-r-e-e-e-n-a-a-a! . . .

Lights dim. Percy begins to join the call, alternating, from behind the clothes rail. He emerges calling and addressing a high and distant Morena. As he talks, the lights come up.

Scene Sixteen

PERCY. Morena! Morena-a-a! Where are you? Come to Albert Street! Come to the Pass Office! We need you here Morena! Ja, Morena, this is the most terrible street in the whole of Johannesburg! Ja, Morena, this is the street where we Black men must come and stand and wait and wait and wait just to get a permit to work in Johannesburg! And if you're lucky enough to get the permit, what happens? You wait and

wait and wait again for the white bosses to come in their
cars to give you work. (*Turns back to Mbongeni.*) But I'm
lucky! I've got six months special! (*Shows his pass-book.*)
Qualified to work in Johannesburg for six months!

MBONGENI. How many months? Eh?

PERCY. Six months!

MBONGENI. Six months? Congratulations. (*Laughs, slaps
Percy's back, shakes his hand.*) Eh! Six month special!

PERCY. Three weeks in a queue!

MBONGENI. But you're still their dog! (*Moves upstage to
urinate, with his back to the audience.*)

PERCY. Aaahh, jealous! You jealous!

MBONGENI. Have you got a job? Have you got school fees for
your children? Have you got money for rent? Have you got
bus fare to come to the Pass Office? Oh, come on man,
we've all got specials but we're still their dogs!

Car sounds.

PERCY (*leaps up*): Hey! There's a car! A white man! (*Moves
to the car at the front edge of the stage, follows it as it
moves across.*) Are you looking for workers, my boss? Ya,
I've got six month special, qualified to work in Johannesburg.

*Mbongeni moves forward trying frantically to distract the
driver. Car sounds continue, actors alternating.*

MBONGENI. Boss, I've got fourteen day special. This is my last
chance. This is my last chance. Take two boys, my boss, two!

PERCY. Messenger boy, tea boy, my boss. One! I make nice
tea for the Madam, my boss. Bush tea, China tea, English
tea! Please, Baba. Lots of experience, Baba. Very good
education, my boss. Please my boss. Standard three, very
good English, Baba.

*Mbongeni's sound of a departing car transforms into a
mocking laugh.*

MBONGENI. I told you, you're still their dog! (*Laughs, mocks.*)
Standard three, bush tea, China tea — where do you get
China tea in Soweto?

PERCY. Aah voetsak! I've got six months special!

On Albert Street.

MBONGENI (*shows Percy his pass-book*): Hey, look at my picture. I look beautiful, heh?

PERCY (*laughs bitterly*): How can you look beautiful in your pass-book?

Car sounds again. Mbongeni rushes forward to the stage edge, follows the car, Percy behind him.

MBONGENI. One! One, my boss! Everything! Sweeper, anything, everything, my boss! Give me anything. Carwash? Yeah, always smiling, my boss. Ag, have you got work for me, my boss? I'm a very good nanny. I look after small white children. I make them tomato sandwich. I take them to school, my boss. Please, my boss. Please.

Car leaves. Mbongeni wanders disconsolately upstage. Percy watches him.

PERCY (*laughing*): Ja! Who's a dog? Don't talk like that! This is South Africa! This is Albert Street. (*Laughs.*) Nanny, nanny, tomato sandwich!

Car sounds again.

BOTH ACTORS (*confusion of requests from each*): Six month special, my boss. Fourteen day special, Baba. This is my last chance. Hey man, this is my corner! Very strong, Baas. Ek donder die kaffers op die plaas. [I beat up the kaffirs on the farm.] One, my boss. Two, my boss. Anything, my boss. Have you got anything for me, Baba?

PERCY. Basie, he's a thief, this one.

MBONGENI. He can't talk Afrikaans, this one, my boss.

PERCY. He's lying, Basie. Hy lieg, my baas!

The third car pulls away.

PERCY (*confronting Mbongeni angrily*): Hey, this is my corner, these are my cars. I've got six months special.

MBONGENI. Hey! Fuck off! I stand where I like, man.

PERCY. You've got fourteen day special. There's your corner.

MBONGENI. Hey! You don't tell me where to stand!

PERCY. You've got fourteen day special. You're not even qualified to be on Albert Street.

MBONGENI. Qualified? Qualified? Wenzani uthath'a ma

shansi hey uthatha ma shansi. [What are you trying to do? You taking chances Hey? You taking chances.]

Mbongeni kicks Percy. Percy turns on him.

PERCY. Baas Piet! Baas Piet! I'll tell Baas Piet you got forgery.

MBONGENI (*mimes picking up stone*). Okay, okay. Call your white boss! I've got friends too!

PERCY. Baas Piet!

MBONGENI (*beckons his friends, wildly picking up stones*): Hey Joe! We Joe! Zwakala — sigunu mfwethu. (*To Percy:*) Angihlali eZola mina — angihlali eMdeni mina — Joe zwakala simenze njalo. [Joe come here — It's happening. (*To Percy:*) I don't live in Zola — I'm not from Mdeni — Joe come here let's work on him.]

Mbongeni quietens, struck by something in the audience.

PERCY (*muttering sulkily*): These are my cars, man. I've got six month special, these are mine. This is my corner — That's the temporal corner! I'll tell Baas Piet!

MBONGENI (*now totally stunned by what he is watching*): Heeey, heeey! Ssh man, ssh.

PERCY (*cautious*): What?

MBONGENI (*indicating the audience*): Morena . . .

PERCY. Aaay, fok off!

MBONGENI. It's Morena — that one there with the white shirt.

PERCY (*doubtfully*): Morena? Ay, nonsense . . . Is it Morena?

MBONGENI. It's him — I saw him in the *Sunday Times* with Bishop Tutu. It's him!

He sidles forward to the edge of the stage. Percy shyly eggs him on.

PERCY. Hey, speak to him.

MBONGENI (*nods with the invisible Morena*): Excuse. Are you not Morena? Yiiiii! Hosanna! Morena!

The actors embrace joyously. Then follow Morena, frantically showing their passes and pleading.

BOTH ACTORS. Morena, look at my pass-book!

PERCY. I've got six month special but I can't find work.

'Morena says no more passes.'

MBONGENI. I've been looking here two months, no work. Take us to heaven, Morena, it's terrible here.

Mbongeni follows Morena. Percy falls behind.

PERCY. Temporary or permanent is okay Morena! (*Silence as Mbongeni converses with Morena. He comes back exhilarated.*) Hey, what does he say?

MBONGENI. He says let us throw away our passes and follow him to Soweto!

PERCY. Hey! He's right! Morena! Morena!

BOTH ACTORS (*sing, exhorting the audience*):
Woza giya nansi inkonyane ye ndlovu —
Aph'amadoda sibabambe sebephelele.
Wozani madoda niyesaba na?

[Come on join this child of an elephant
Where are the men? Let us face them!
Come men, are you afraid?]

PERCY (*under the song*): Morena says throw away your passes and follow him to Soweto.

MBONGENI. We are not pieces of paper, man! We are men!

PERCY. Ja! Let them know our faces as Morena knows our faces!

MBONGENI. Morena says no more passes!

PERCY. Ja!!

MBONGENI. We don't have numbers any more!

PERCY. Ja!

MBONGENI. Let them look at our faces to know that we are men.

PERCY. Ja! When we follow Morena we walk as one!

The actors throw away their passes and their song transforms into train sounds.

Scene Seventeen

The actors mime standing beside each other at a train window. They wave to people outside.

PERCY. Hey madoda! Sanibona madoda! May God bless them! Ja, you've got a very good imagination. I really like your stories. But you must go to church sometimes — Hey, there's a train coming! (*Looks to one side.*)

Flurry of their faces and noises as they mime watching adjoining train pass. Then they pull their windows up. Siren. Mbongeni moves downstage. Percy stands on a box, begins Regina Mundi Song:

Somlandela — somlandela u Morena
Somlandela yonke indawo
Somlandela — somlandela u Morena
Lapho eyakhona somlandela.

[We shall follow — we shall follow Morena
We shall follow him everywhere
We shall follow — we shall follow Morena
Where-ever he leads — we shall follow.]

While the song continues:

MBONGENI (*joyous siren*): Ja, madoda, hundreds of thousands will gather at the Regina Mundi Church in the heart of Soweto. And people will sing and dance. There will be bread for all. And wine for all. Our people will be left in peace, because there will be too many of us and the whole world will be watching. And people will go home to their beds. (*He joins in the song for a few phrases.*) These will be days of joy. Auntie Dudu will find chicken legs in her rubbish bin, and whole cabbages. And amadoda — our men — will be offered work at the Pass Office. The barber will be surrounded by white tiles. The young meat-seller will wear a nice new uniform and go to school, and we will all go to Morena for our blessings. (*Song subsides. Percy lies on boxes as sleeping woman. Lights dim.*) And then . . . the government will begin to take courage again . . . The police and the army will assemble from all parts of the country . . . And one night, police dogs will move in as they have done before. There will be shouts at night and bangings on the door . . .

PERCY (*banging on a box*): Hey! Open up, it's the police! Maak die deur oop! Polisie!

MBONGENI (*ducking down by the boxes as if hiding beside a bed*): . . . There will be sounds of police vans and the crying of women and their babies.

PERCY (*turns over on the boxes as an old woman waking in bed, starts crying and calling in Zulu*): We Jabulani, hayi-bo-hey-hey-we-Nonoza, akenivule bo nanka amaphoyisa esesihlasele, we Thoko akenivule bo. Auw-Nkosi-Yami, ezingane ze-Black Power! [Hey, Jabulani, Hey no, hey-hey, Nonoza, open the door can't you hear the police are here. They've come to attack us. Thoko, please open the door. Oh my God, these children of Black Power!]

He goes to open the door. Throughout Mbongeni tries to stop him.

MBONGENI. Sssh Mama! Tula Mama! Mama! Mama! Leave the door! (*Mbongeni gives up, stands silent, transfixed, hiding.*) They'll start surrounding our homes at night. And some of our friends will be caught by stray bullets. There will be road-blocks at every entrance to Soweto, and Regina Mundi Church will be full of tear-gas smoke! Then life will go on as before.

He throws his arms up in the air in disgust, cries out.

Scene Eighteen

Lights flash on. Bright daylight. Coronation Brickyard. Mbongeni, as Zuluboy, is singing:

MBONGENI (*singing*):
Akuntombi lokhu kwabulala ubhuti ngesibumbu kuyamsondeza. [This is no woman. She killed my brother with a fuck and she never lets him go.]

(*He calls out towards the street*): Hey Angelina — sweetheart! Why are you walking down the street? Come here to Coronation Brickyard! Zuluboy is waiting for you with a nice present! (*Points to his genitals, laughing*).

PERCY (*enters as Bobbejaan — Baboon — Zuluboy's fellow brickyard worker*): Hey! Zuluboy, forget about women. Start the machine!

Mbongeni sings on.

PERCY. Hey! The white man is watching us. Boss Kom is standing by the window! Start the machine.

He makes machine sounds as he attempts to start it. He pulls the starter cord abortively, flies backwards across the yard.

MBONGENI (*laughs*): Hey Bobbejaan! Start the machine!

PERCY. You laugh and I must do all this work! I'll tell Baas Kom. Baas Kom! Basie! Baas Kom!

MBONGENI. Ssshhhhhh! Bobbejaan! Bobbejaan . . . ssh — I want to tell you a secret.

PERCY. What secret?

MBONGENI (*whispers*): We don't have to work so hard any more. Because Morena, the saviour, is coming here.

PERCY. Huh? Morena here? Hau! Baas Kom!

MBONGENI. Hau, no Bobbejaan! Listen — I was there on Thursday by the Jan Smuts Airport. We were delivering bricks. People were coming with taxis, bikes, trains, trucks, others on foot. There were many people, Bobbejaan. They were singing and crying and laughing and dancing and sweating and this other woman was shouting: Morena, give me bread for my baby. The other woman was shouting: Morena, my son is in detention. The other man: Morena, give me a special permit to work in Johannesburg city. The little girl, standing next to me: Morena, give me a lollipop. The big fat Zulu — the driver from Zola Hostel — Morena, give me a Chevrolet Impala! And me — I was there too —

PERCY. What did you say?

MBONGENI. Morena, come to Coronation Brickyard tomorrow morning! And he's coming here.

PERCY. To Coronation Brickyard? Morena?

MBONGENI. Hau — Bobbejaan, at the wedding, long ago — ten thousand years ago — he take a bucket of water, he make wine.

PERCY (*smugly*): Ja, everybody knows that!

MBONGENI. He take one fish, he make fish for everybody! Fried fish!

In the brickyard: Zuluboy and Bobbejaan.

PERCY. Hau!

MBONGENI. He take one loaf of brown bread, he make the whole bakery! Here at Coronation Brickyard, you will see wonders. He will take one brick, number one brick, and throw it up in the air. And it will fall down on our heads, a million bricks like manna from heaven!

PERCY. Hey! You're talking nonsense. Morena? Here at Coronation Bricks? Start the machine. I'll tell Baas Kom!

Percy goes off. Mbongeni begins rolling a cigarette, singing his Zuluboy's song. Percy, as Baas Kom with pink nose and white dust-coat, enters quietly from behind the clothes rail and creeps up on him. Mbongeni spits, just missing Percy who leaps back.

MBONGENI. Oh, sorry, Boss. Sorry, sorry . . . (*He runs to start the machine.*)

PERCY. Sis! Where were you brought up?

MBONGENI. Sorry Boss!

PERCY. Ja Zuluboy! And what are you sitting around for?

MBONGENI. Sorry, Boss. Sorry.

PERCY. Are you waiting for Morena?

MBONGENI. No, Boss. No.

PERCY. Ja, I've been listening. I've been watching. You're waiting for Morena. Ja. Did you not listen to the Prime Minister on the radio today?

MBONGENI. I don't have a radio, Boss.

PERCY. We don't like Morena anymore. And everybody who's waiting for Morena is getting fired.

MBONGENI. Oh, very good, Boss. Me? I'm Zuluboy — ten thousand bricks in one day!

PERCY. Ja. Where's Bobbejaan?

MBONGENI (*attempting to start the machine*): He's gone to the toilet.

PERCY. Call him. Call him, quickly!

MBONGENI. Hey! Bobbejaan! (*He makes motor sounds as the machine kicks over but does not 'take'.*) Bobbejaan!

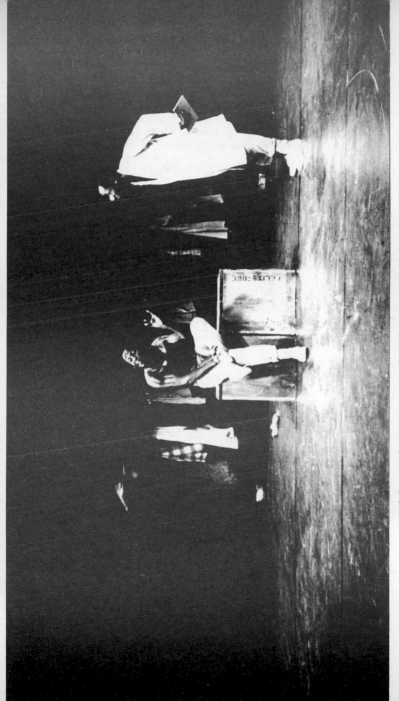

Zuluboy and Baas Kom: 'And what are you sitting around for?'

PERCY (*still as Baas Kom, with Mbongeni watching over his shoulder*): Now listen. I want two thousand bricks for Boss Koekemoer. Two thousand bricks for Baas Pretorius. Two thousand bricks for Mrs Dawson. (*Mbongeni indicates his pleasure in Mrs Dawson. Percy cautions him:*) Zuluboy! Six thousand bricks for Boss Van der Westhuizen. Two thousand bricks for Boss Koekemoer. Two thousand bricks for Baas Pretorius. Two thousand bricks for Mrs Dawson.

MBONGENI. Baas, sorry, I'm confused.

PERCY. What confused? What confused? You're bloody lazy, man! See to these orders and push the truck. (*He indicates the truck on the side of the stage.*)

MBONGENI. Hey! This truck is too heavy, Baas!

PERCY. Get other people!

MBONGENI. People have gone to lunch.

PERCY. Get Bobbejaan!

MBONGENI. Ten thousand bricks, Boss!

PERCY. Hey! Get Bobbejaan!

MBONGENI. Bobbejaan! Uyahamba laphe khaya. [They'll fire you.] Bobbejaan! (*Mumbling:*) Two thousand bricks Mrs Dawson . . . Hau! (*Laughs with pleasure.*) Mrs Dawson! Ten thousand brick Baas van Des-des-destuizen . . . Too much! (*He starts the engine. Engine 'takes'. Mbongeni shouts:*) Bobbejaan!

PERCY (*off-stage, as Bobbejaan*): I'm coming, man! (*He enters.*) Hey, hey. Where's Morena?

MBONGENI. No, Morena. Hey, shovel the sand. Baas Kom is firing everybody that's waiting for Morena.

PERCY (*laughing*): Ja! I've been telling you! Hey, bring down the pot. (*They alternate shovel and motor sounds, as they mime shovelling. Mbongeni begins to sing and dance his Zuluboy song.*) Hey, stop dancing. Stop dancing!

MBONGENI. Hey! I am boss-boy here!

Mbongeni switches off the machine.

PERCY. Lunch time!

MBONGENI. No Bobbejaan. First push the truck.

PERCY. Hau! Ten thousand bricks! Hau! Lunch time!

MBONGENI. Baas Kom said, push the truck! Get Bobbejaan, push the truck. PUSH!

Percy joins him reluctantly. They start to chant while they mime pushing the heavy truck.

BOTH (*chanting*):
Woza kanye-kanye! [Come together!]
Abelungu oswajini! [Whites are swines!]
Basibiza ngo-damn! [They call us damns!]

Woza kanye-kanye! [Come together!]
Abelungu oswayini! [Whites are swines!]
Basibiza ngo-damn! [They call us damns!]

They finally stop, exhausted.

PERCY (*holding his back, moaning*): Oh, oh, oh, yii, yii! Lunch time! Hayi ndiva kuthi qhu. [My back is breaking.]

MBONGENI. Hayi suka unamanga. [Hey you lie.] (*He squats to examine the truck.*) It has gone too far. Reverse!

PERCY. Reverse?! Reverse?

Muttering, he joins Mbongeni. They pull the truck back again, chanting.

BOTH (*chanting*):
Woza emuva! [Come reverse!]
Phenduka ayi. [Change now.]
Abelungu oswayini! [Whites are swines!]
Basibiza ngo-damn! [They call us damns!]

PERCY. Hayi. (*Percy goes off.*)

MBONGENI. Bobbejaan, come back, it stuck in ditch.

PERCY (*off-stage*): Hayi, xelel'ubaas Kom ukuba sifuna i-increase. [Tell Baas Kom we want increase;]

MBONGENI. We . . . kuyintekentekana lokhu okuwu-Bobbejaan. [Hey man, Bobbejaan is too weak.] Come back, Bobbejaan! Uyahamba laphe khaya. [They'll fire you.] Where's my cigarette? (*Mimes lighting a cigarette. Talks to himself, starts praise-chant.*)

PERCY (*enters as Baas Kom*): And now? And now? (*Mocking praise-chant:*) Aaay, hakela, hakela. What the bloody hell is that? Huh? Push the truck! Come!

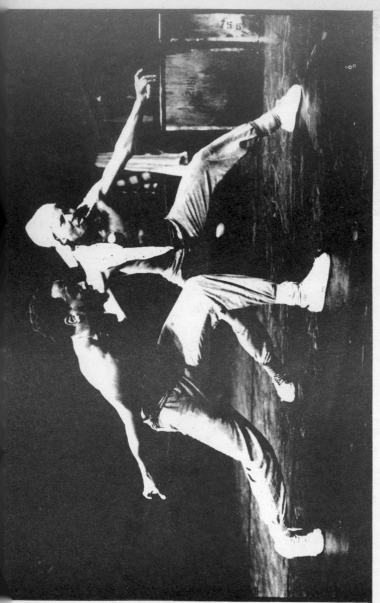

Pulling the truck.

MBONGENI. Having rest, baas. Still smoking.

PERCY. Do you think I pay you for smoking? (*Glances at the truck*.) Hey, push the truck!

MBONGENI. We pushed the truck! Ten thousand bricks! Boss, there's too much work for two people. Me and Bobbejaan start the engine. Me and Bobbejaan shovel the sand. Me and Bobbejaan load the bricks. Me and Bobbejaan push the truck! Aaay suka! We need other people!

PERCY. There's no jobs!

MBONGENI. There *is* jobs!!! Ten thousand bricks! This morning there were many people at the gates standing there looking for work. And you chased them away!

PERCY. Zuluboy, you're getting cheeky, huh?

MBONGENI. I'm not getting cheeky. It's true.

PERCY. Ja! I'm cutting down your salary. I think you're getting too much. Ja! Ja!

MBONGENI. The boss can't cut salary.

PERCY. Ek gaan dit doen! [I'm going to do it.]

MBONGENI. That's not showing sympathy for another man. The cost of living is too high. There is too much inflation.

PERCY. Zuluboy! Zuluboy! You sit around waiting for Morena and then you come and tell me about the cost of living? You talk about inflation? What do you know about inflation? I've got you here, just here. One more mistake, once more cheeky, and you're fired!

MBONGENI. Okay. All right boss. Let's talk business like two people.

PERCY (*bangs on the box*): He-ey! Push the truck, man!

MBONGENI (*furious, bangs on the box. Percy retreats towards his office space*): Hey! You must listen nice when another man talks!

PERCY. Okay. Talk, talk. (*Mbongeni advances.*) No — talk over there, talk over there!

MBONGENI (*backs away*): All right. Okay, okay. The people want increase. Where's the money for the people?

PERCY. Increase?

MBONGENI. Increase!

PERCY. Don't I give you free food? Free boarding and lodging?

MBONGENI. The people don't like your free food! They want money. There is too big families to support. Too many children.

PERCY. I don't give a damn about your too many children. Don't you know about family planning?

MBONGENI. Family planning? What is that?

PERCY. Don't you know that you must not have too many children? You must have two, three, and stop your fuck-fuck nonsense! Too many pic-a-ninnies! Too many black kaffir babies all over the country. (*Sharing this with the audience:*) Their kaffir babies cry 'Waaaaa! Waaaaa!' Just like too many piccaninny dogs!

MBONGENI (*threatening*): Hey!

PERCY. Zuluboy!

MBONGENI. Whose children cry 'Waaa, waaa!'?

PERCY. Zuluboy!

MBONGENI. Whose children is piccaninny dogs?

PERCY. Bring your pass-book!

MBONGENI. Why?

PERCY. You're fired! Bring your pass-book. I'm signing you off.

MBONGENI. You can't sign me off!

PERCY. I'm calling the police! I'm calling the government buses and I'm sending you back to your homelands. Ek stuur julle na julle fokken verdomde, donorse, bliksemse plase toe! [I'm sending you to your fucking, cursed, useless farms.] You don't like my work? You don't like my food! Go back to your bladdy farms! Go starve on your bladdy farms!

MBONGENI. I must starve?

PERCY. Ja!

MBONGENI. My children must starve?

PERCY. Ja!

MBONGENI. Go on strike!!!

PERCY. Hey! Bring your pass-book!

MBONGENI (*pulls out his knobkerrie from behind the box*): Here's my pass-book!

PERCY. Zuluboy!

MBONGENI (*advancing*): Here's my pass-book.

PERCY (*ducking behind the rack of clothes at the back of the stage*): Bobbejaan!

MBONGENI. Here's my pass-book! Stay away — hlala phansi wena ngane ka Ngema. Hlala wena ngane ka Madlokovu — hlala. Wena dlula bedlana inkunzi engena mona, hlala phansi mfana — Hlala!! Pho — kuhlala ba. [Stay away — sit down you son of Ngema. Sit down son of Madlokovu. Sit. You fuck and you never feel jealous. Sit down great son. Sit. So who am I — the greatest!] (*Mutters to himself:*) Stay away. Go on strike. My children cry 'Waa waa'. (*Suddenly he sees Morena approaching. He wipes the sweat from his eyes, shakes his head in disbelief. Falls to his knees.*) Hey, Hey! Morena! So you've come to Coronation Bricks! Come, Morena. Did you listen to the radio today? Everybody's waiting for you, and everybody is fired. Come, sit down here, Morena. (*Offers a box.*) Sit down. Sit down Morena. (*Calls out:*) Bobbejaan!

PERCY (*entering as Bobbejaan, angrily*): Hau! One minute 'Bobbejaan!' One minute 'Bobbejaan!' (*He sees Morena, stops complaining and turns away shyly.*)

MBONGENI (*laughs*): Bobbejaan, who is this? Who is this!!!

PERCY (*backs away smiling shyly*): Hey. I don't know him. Who is it?

MBONGENI. Who is this? I win the bet. Give ten rands.

PERCY. Who is he?

MBONGENI. Give ten rands!

PERCY. Who is he?

MBONGENI. Morena!

PERCY. Hey! Morena?!

MBONGENI. He's from heaven. He has come now. He landed at Jan Smuts Airport on Thursday by the airline from Jerusalem.

Talking to Morena.

PERCY. Hey Morena! (*Clapping hands*.) I saw your picture in the paper. Morena, I could not believe you're coming. I thought you're coming back by the clouds. (*He sits on the floor*.)

MBONGENI. The clouds are too hot now. It's summer. He flies air-conditioned. Excuse, Morena, this is Bobbejaan. Bobbejaan, shake hands with Morena. (*Percy stands, embarrassed, backs away*.) Shake hands with the Son of God! Shake hands, Bobbejaan! (*Percy ducks behind the Zuluboy on the box. Zuluboy laughs*.) Bobbejaan is shy! We are working together here, Morena. When I say, 'Morena, come to Coronation Brickyard', I mean you must make bricks like you make bread and wine long ago. I mean you must make bricks to fall down like manna from heaven —

PERCY. Like you made fried fish!

MBONGENI. Ja! But now, I say no! Stay away! No! You must not make bricks for Coronation Brickyard! You must go on strike like me and Bobbejaan! Angithi Bobbejaan? [Isn't it so, Bobbejaan?] We work hard here. We sweat. Sweating for one man!

PERCY. Boss Koekemoer!

MBONGENI. Every Friday, Boss Koekemoer, seven thousand bricks —

PERCY. Boss Pretorius!

MBONGENI. Boss Pretorius ten thousand bricks!

PERCY. Van de Westhuizen!

MBONGENI. Boss Van-des-destuizen, eleven thousand bricks! Where do we stay?

PERCY. In a tin!

MBONGENI. In a tin! Like sardine fish!

PERCY. In a tin, Morena!

MBONGENI. Where do the bricks go to!? The bricks go to make a big house, six rooms, for two people. A white man and his wife! Angithi Bobbejaan? [Isn't it so, Bobbejaan?] Our fingers are breaking Morena! Is nie good kanjalo man. [That's not good like that, man.]

PERCY. Ten thousand bricks!

MBONGENI. Ten thousand bricks! Me and Bobbejaan must push the truck. Aaay suka! Stay away! No bricks for Coronation Bricks! (*He puts out his cigarette and clears his nose — to Percy's embarrassment.*) Are you hungry, Morena? Are you hungry? I've got nice food for you. I've got a packet of chips. (*Mimes.*) It's very good, this one. There's lots of vinegar and salt — I bought them from the shop just around the corner.

PERCY. That's potatoes, Morena.

MBONGENI. I've got half-brown bread. Whole-wheat. You made this long ago, huh? I've been telling Bobbejaan, you made plenty in the wedding — He's got power, this one! (*Mimes.*) This is Coca-cola, Morena.

PERCY. It's cold drink.

MBONGENI. For quenching thirst.

PERCY. Ha, Morena, there's no Coca-cola in heaven?

MBONGENI. What do you drink up there?

They listen, then laugh uproariously.

PERCY. These two!

MBONGENI. You and your father! Skelm! [Mischief-makers!]

He mimes opening a coke bottle.

PERCY (*looks upstage, then calls in Baas Kom's voice, as if from off-stage*): Bobbejaan! (*Then as Bobbejaan again:*) Baas Kom! Morena, I must go! One minute 'Bobbejaan!' One minute 'Bobbejaan!' (*Going off:*) Hey Zuluboy, I want my chips!

MBONGENI (*drinks from the mimed coke bottle, burps, offers it to Morena*): Yabhodla ingane yenZule ukuba okungu — MSuthu ngabe kudala kuzinyele. [There burps the son of a Zulu; if it was a Sotho he would be shitting.] Did you hear that man who was shouting 'Bobbejaan'? That's our white boss. Boss Kom. He's not good. But don't worry . . .

PERCY (*off-stage in Baas Kom's voice*): Bobbejaan!

MBONGENI. Lots of vinegar . . .

PERCY (*enters as Baas Kom, stops at sight of Morena*): En nou! En nou? Who is this? Who is sitting around eating lunch with my kaffirs? That's why you're getting cheeky, hey? Ja, you sit around and have lunch with terrorists!

MBONGENI. Hau! He's not a terrorist, Baas! He's a big man from heaven!

PERCY. This man is a communist, jong! Ek het van jou nonsense gehoor. Die hele land praat van jou. [I've heard of your nonsense. The whole country is talking about you.]

MBONGENI. Excuse. He cannot understand Afrikaans.

PERCY. What? Cannot understand Afrikaans?

MBONGENI. Right.

PERCY. Cannot understand Afrikaans? Stay where you are! (*Retreats to his office behind the clothes.*) I'm calling the police. Fuckin' agitator!

MBONGENI. Aay suka!! Don't worry, Morena, don't worry. (*He proffers the coke bottle.*) He does not know who you are. He does not know who your father is.

PERCY (*as Baas Kom, offstage*): Hello? Hello? Lieutenant Venter? Ja! Now listen here. There's a terrorist here who's making trouble with my kaffirs. Ek sê daar's 'n uitlander hier wat kak maak met my kaffirs. [I say there's a foreigner here who's making shit with my kaffirs.] Ja. Hello? Hello? Ag die fuckin' telephone! Bobbejaan! (*As Bobbejaan:*) Ja, Basie? (*As Baas Kom:*) Kom, kom, kom. (*As Bobbejaan:*) Ja, Basie? (*As Baas Kom:*) You see that man eating with Zuluboy? (*As Bobbejaan:*) Ja, Basie. (*As Baas Kom:*) He's a terrorist! (*As Bobbejaan:*) A terrorist, Basie? That's Morena! (*As Baas Kom:*) It's not Morena — Now listen here. Listen carefully. I'm writing down this message. You take this message to the police station and I'm going to give you a very nice present. A ten rand increase, okay? (*As Bobbejaan:*) Ja, thank you Basie, thank you Basie. (*As Baas Kom:*) Ja, go straight to the police station and don't tell Zuluboy. (*As Bobbejaan:*) Ja Basie, ja. (*As Baas Kom:*) Go to the police station and you get the ten rand increase!

MBONGENI. Did you hear that, Morena? (*He listens.*) What? Forgive a man seventy times seventy-seven? Aikhona Morena! This is South Africa. We fight! Bobbejaan is very dangerous. (*Listens to Morena.*) Okay, you win. Wait and see, Morena.

PERCY (*enters as Bobbejaan, putting on his shirt*): Morena,
   I'm going to the shop, just around the corner.

MBONGENI. Bobbejaan, your chips are here.

PERCY. Give them to Morena.

MBONGENI. Morena is not hungry.

PERCY. Eat them yourself.

MBONGENI. I'm not hungry either. Where are you going,
   Bobbejaan?

PERCY. To the shop!

MBONGENI. Why, Bobbejaan?

PERCY. I'm going to buy hot-dogs for Baas Kom.

MBONGENI. Where's the money?

PERCY. I've got it here.

MBONGENI. Show it to me.

PERCY. Why?

MBONGENI. Ja. You Judas, Bobbejaan!

PERCY. What are you talking about?

MBONGENI. You betray Morena, Bobbejaan.

PERCY. Haw! Morena, do you hear that?

MBONGENI. Bobbejaan, you betray Morena, Bobbejaan!
   You Judas, Bobbejaan!

PERCY. I'm going to buy hot-dogs for Baas Kom!

MBONGENI. You . . . you . . . you take a message to the police.
   And you get ten rands increase Bobbejaan!

PERCY. Aay Morena. Morena, do you hear that?

MBONGENI. Morena, shhh. Keep quiet. This is South Africa.
   Ten rands increase (*He reaches for the knobkerrie.*)

PERCY. Baas Kom! (*He runs off.*)

MBONGENI (*mimes his knobkerrie being grabbed by Morena*):
   Morena, leave it! Leave it! Morena! Morena, leave it! Morena!
   He has run away now. Bobbejaan, sodibana nawe wena.
   [Bobbejaan, you and I will meet again.] A man hits this cheek
   you give him the other. Aikhona, Morena! They're calling the
   police to arrest you now! Okay, come. Let me hide you there

Zuluboy's war dance.

by the trees — Quickly — (*Siren sounds. He stops.*) There's
one, two, three . . . there's thirteen police cars. Huh? Forgive
them, they do not know what they are doing? Aikhona,
Morena! They know! They know! (*He sings and performs a
Zulu war dance, which ends with him thrusting his
knobkerrie again and again at the audience in attack.*)

Qobolela njomane kandaba heya-he
soze sibajahe abelungu he ya he.

[Be ready you horses of the black warriors
Time will come when we'll chase these whites away.]

Scene Nineteen

*The lights come up on the actors wearing military hats and pink
noses. Percy has a bloody bandage under his hat.*

MBONGENI. Address! Ssshhhooo! Attention!

   They drill in unison.

PERCY (*saluting*): Reporting sir! John Vorster Squad, sir!

MBONGENI. What have you to report, Sergeant?

PERCY. Operation Coronation, sir!

MBONGENI. Meaning, Sergeant?

PERCY. We have finally captured Morena, sir!

MBONGENI. You've what? Attention! One-two-three-one-
two-three-one! (*They march to each other, shake hands.*)
Excellent, Sergeant! Excellent!

PERCY. Thank you, sir.

MBONGENI. And now, what's happened to your head, Sergeant?

PERCY. A mad Zulu, sir.

MBONGENI. A mad Zulu?

PERCY. Yes sir. He struck me with the branch of a tree, sir.

MBONGENI. A branch of a tree?

PERCY. They call it a knobkerrie, sir.

MBONGENI. Ah! When, Sergeant?

PERCY. During Operation Coronation, sir.

MBONGENI. You mean Morena was with a bunch of mad Zulus?

PERCY. No, sir.

MBONGENI. What does he mean, this stupid Sergeant?

PERCY. He was with one mad Zulu, sir!

MBONGENI. One mad Zulu?

PERCY. Yes, sir!

MBONGENI. And how many men did you have, Sergeant?

PERCY. Thirty, sir!

MBONGENI. And where are they now, Sergeant?

PERCY. In hospital, sir!

MBONGENI. And the mad Zulu?

PERCY. He got away, sir!

MBONGENI. God! Wat gaan aan?! [God! What's going on?!] Where is Morena now, Sergeant?

PERCY (*pointing proudly above the audience*): He's upstairs, above us, sir. On the tenth floor of John Vorster Square Prison, sir!

MBONGENI. Aaaahhh! (*Looking up.*) And you've provided ample guard, Sergeant?

PERCY. Yes, sir. One hundred and twenty, sir.

MBONGENI (*moving forward, watching the tenth floor, mesmerised*): Are you sure he's on the tenth floor, Sergeant?

PERCY (*following his gaze nervously*): Yes, sir.

MBONGENI. Then what is that I see?

PERCY (*moving behind him, also mesmerised, both eye-lines travelling above the audience*): I'm sorry sir.

MBONGENI. Why are you sorry, Sergeant?

PERCY. I see two men floating, sir.

MBONGENI. Then why are you sorry, Sergeant?

PERCY. I'm afraid one of them is Morena, sir.

MBONGENI (*moving in, nose-to-nose, menacingly*): Precisely,

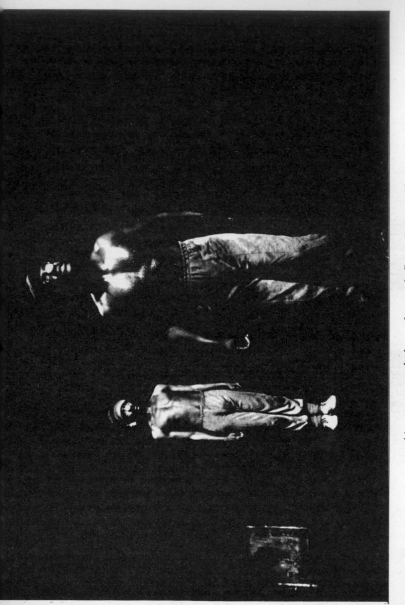

'Are you sure he's on the tenth floor, Sergeant?'

Sergeant! And-who-is-the-other?

PERCY. The Angel Gabriel, sir.

MBONGENI (*despairing*): Ha! Gabriel!

PERCY. I'm sorry, sir. I never thought of air flight, sir.

MBONGENI. Eeeeeiiiii! One-two-three-four-one-four! Attention! Dismissed, Sergeant!

Scene Twenty

Lights find both actors travelling beside each other on a train.

MBONGENI (*laughing*): Jaaa. And where do we go from there? After a miracle like flying men, I'm telling you the government will be real nervous. And they won't start nonsense with him for a long time. In fact, they will try very hard to please Morena. He will be taken to all the nice places in the country. Like the game reserve where he can lie down with a leopard and a lamb. (*They cuddle.*) And then — (*They mime a high-speed lift.*) — they will take him right up to the high spots of Johannesburg City — Panorama Wimpy Bar, Carlton Centre, fiftieth floor! And then, on a Thursday they will take him down — (*They mime going down, pink noses on their foreheads like miners' lamps.*) — the gold mines to watch. (*They mime deafening drills.*) And then, on a Sunday the mine dancers. (*They perform a short dance routine.*) And — (*Hand to ear.*) — aah, the government gardens in Pretoria. (*Doves cooing.*) And then, they will take him on a trip to SUN CITY — (*Stage radiantly light.*) — THE LAS VEGAS OF SOUTH AFRICA, where they will build him a holy suite and President Lucas Mangope, the puppet, will offer him the key to the homeland of Bophutatswana! And then, what will happen? They will take him past the good-time girls. (*Standing on a box, Percy mimes.*) And the gambling machines. (*Percy transforms into a one-armed bandit, Mbongeni works him, wins triumphantly.*) And when television cameras turn on him, will he be smiling? Will he be joyous? No. He'll be crying. And when all the people shout —

BOTH: Speech! Morena, speech!

The mine dancers.

The one-armed bandit.

MBONGENI. — Morena will say, 'No.'

PERCY (*miming holding a mike*): No, speak up.

MBONGENI. No! Morena will say, what key is this? What place is this? This place where old people weep over the graves of children? How has it happened? How has it been permitted? I've passed people with burning mouths. People buying water in a rusty piece of tin, and beside them I see people swimming in a lake that they have made from water that is here!

PERCY. Be careful, there are police spies here.

MBONGENI. What spies? Morena will say, I pass people who sit in dust and beg for work that will buy them bread. And on the other side I see people who are living in gold and glass and whose rubbish bins are loaded with food for a thousand mouths.

PERCY. Hey! That's not your business. There are security police, man.

MBONGENI. What security police? Morena will say, I see families torn apart, I see mothers without sons, children without fathers, and wives who have no men! Where are the men? Aph'amadoda madoda? [Where are the men?] And people will say, Ja, Morena, it's this bladdy apartheid. It's those puppets, u Mangope! u Matanzima! u Sebe! Together with their white Pretoria masters. They separate us from our wives, from our sons and daughters! And women will say, Morena there's no work in the homelands. There's no food. They divide us from our husbands and they pack them into hostels like men with no names, men with no lives! And Morena will say, come to me, you who are divided from your families. Let us go to the cities where your husbands work. We will find houses where you can live together and we will talk to those who you fear! What country is this? (*Spits on ground.*)

Percy starts to sing and march on the spot. Mbongeni joins him. They mime carrying a banner.

BOTH ACTORS (*sing a Zulu song and march*):
Oyini oyini madoda
Oyini oyini madoda
Sibona ntoni uma sibon'u Mangope

'What country is this?'

Siboni sell-out uma sibon'u Mangope
Sibona ntoni uma sibon'u Gatsha
Siboni puppet uma sibon'u Gatsha
Khulula khulula Morena
Khulula khulula Morena
Sibona ntoni nang'u Matanzima
Sibon'u mbulali nang'u Matanzima

[What is this, what is this men
What is this, what is this men
What do we see when we see Mangope
We see a sell-out when we see Mangope
What do we see when we see Gatsha
We see a puppet when we see Gatsha
Help us — Help us Morena
Help us — Help us Morena
What do we see — there is Matanzima
We see a killer when we see Matanzima.]

PERCY (*interrupted*): Hey! Tear gas!

*They struggle, continuing the song, throwing stones,
sounding sirens, dogs barking.
Lights go down as they are subdued.*

BOTH. Morena-a-a-a! Morena-a-a-a!

Scene Twenty-one

Spotlight finds Percy as Prime Minister, pink nose, spectacles.

PERCY. My people, as your Prime Minister I must warn you
that we stand alone in the face of total onslaught. Our
enemies will stop at nothing, even to the extent of sending
a cheap communist magician to pose as the Morena, and
undermine the security of our nation. But let me assure
you that this cheap impostor is safely behind bars, from which
he cannot fly. Peace and security have returned to our
lovely land.

Scene Twenty-two

Lights come up on Mbongeni squatting on a box, wrapped in a prisoner's blanket.

MBONGENI (*knocking*): Cell number six! Morena! (*Knocking.*) Cell number six! Morena! Bad luck, hey! I hear they got you again. They tell me you're in solitary confinement just like us. From Sun City to Robben Island! (*Laughs ruefully.*) You've made us famous, Morena. The whole world is talking about us. Hey bayasiteya labedana bamabhunu man! [Hey they are riding us these white boys.] Morena, I sit here just like you with this one light bulb and only the Bible to read! Ja! And the New Testament tells me about you, and your family, and your thoughts. But why do they give us your book to read, Morena? They must be bladdy mad, Morena. This book only proves how mad they are. Listen. (*Knocking.*) Cell number six! For people like us, to be locked here like this is just rubbish. So what do you want here? What does your father know? What does he say? Come on Morena, man! (*Knocking.*) Cell number six! You've got all the power! How can you let these things happen? How can you just sit there like that, Morena? Okay, okay, I know you don't like miracles, but these are bladdy hard times, Morena. Morena, I must tell you, now that I've gone into your book, I really like you, Morena. But I'm getting bladdy disappointed. How long must we wait for you to do something? Morena, I must tell you, I'm among those who have stopped waiting. One day we'll have to help you! Phambiti neri-hondo! [Power to the people!] Can you hear me Morena? Cell number six!! (*'Sarie Marais' being whistled off-stage. Knocking more cautiously:*) Cell number six!! Morena! Morena . . . Cell number six . . .

Scene Twenty-three

Percy enters whistling 'Sarie Marais'. He is a soldier, pink nose, camouflage hat. Mimes carrying rifle.

MBONGENI (*enters similarly dressed*): Two three! Morning Corporal!

'Can you hear me Morena? Cell number six!'

PERCY. Morning Sergeant!

MBONGENI. How are things going, Corporal? (*He rests on a box.*)

PERCY. I'm tired, Sergeant.

MBONGENI. Oh, God. To be a guard on bladdy Robben Island!

PERCY. Ja, ever since they brought Morena out here to Robben Island everything has been upside down.

MBONGENI. All those bladdy interviews, that's what's killing us!

PERCY. I'm sick of having my photograph taken.

MBONGENI. I know. The next photographer I see, I shoot to kill!

PERCY. Daily News.

MBONGENI. Sunday Times.

PERCY. Time Life.

MBONGENI. Pravda.

PERCY. London Observer.

MBONGENI. New York Times.

PERCY. All those bladdy communists!

MBONGENI. You know, I got a letter from a woman in Sweden. She saw my photograph in her newspaper. And my wife was chasing me with a frying pan! I told her I never knew the woman, but she didn't believe me.

PERCY. I wish they had kept him in John Vorster Square or Pretoria Central.

MBONGENI. Come on, Corporal. You know what happened at John Vorster Square. Gabriel got him out of there in ten seconds flat! Only Robben Island has got the right kind of AA missiles.

PERCY. AA? What is that?

MBONGENI. Anti-Angel.

PERCY. Anti-Angel? I never heard of that!

MBONGENI. He'll never get away from Robben Island!

PERCY (*distracted, points into the audience*): Hey! Sergeant!

In the helicopter.

What's that you said? Just look over there! Just look over there!!!

MBONGENI (*moves lazily toward him singing 'Sarie Marais'*):
My Sarie Marais is so ver van my hart . . . (*Suddenly he looks into the audience, horrified.*) God! Hey! Fire! Fire!

They riddle the audience with machine-gun fire.

PERCY. Call helicopter control, quick!!!

MBONGENI. Hello? Hello? Radio 1254 CB? Over. Hello? Radio 1254 . . .

Scene Twenty-four

Lights reduce to spot-light the boxes. Actors turn their hat brims up. Mbongeni spins his hand above his head. Helicopter sounds. They are in a helicopter, looking down.

PERCY (*mimes radio*): Radio 1254 CB receiving, over. What? That's impossible! Are you sure? Okay, over and out. Hey, what do you see down below?

MBONGENI (*miming binoculars*): Oh, it's a beautiful day down below. Birds are flying, swimmers are swimming, waves are waving. Hey! Morena's walking on water to Cape Town! Ag shame! His feet must be freezing! Hey, I wish I had my camera here!

PERCY. This must be the miracle of the decade!

MBONGENI. Ag, I always forget my camera!

PERCY. Down! Down! Radio 1254 CB receiving, over. Yes, we've got him. Yeah, what? Torpedo? Oh no, have a heart! He's not even disturbing the waves! Ja, I wish you could see him, he looks amazing!

MBONGENI (*nodding frenetically into mike*): Ja jong, ja! [Yes man, yes!]

PERCY. What? Bomb Morena? Haven't you heard what they say? You start with Morena and it's worse than an atom bomb! Over and out! Hey, this is a shit bladdy job! You pull the chain.

MBONGENI. No, you!

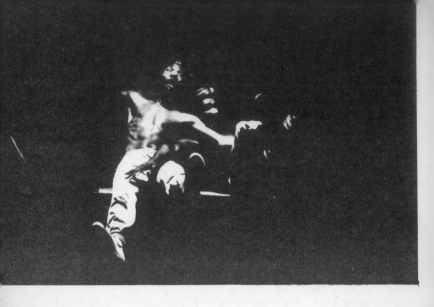

'A terrible explosion. . .'

PERCY. No! You pull the chain!

MBONGENI. No, man!

PERCY. This man is mos' happy, why blow him up?

MBONGENI. No come on, come on. Fair deal! Eenie, meenie, minie moe. Vang a kaffir by the toe. As hy shrik, let him go. Eenie, meenie, minie, moe! It's you!

PERCY. Okay! This is the last straw! I think I'm resigning tomorrow!

MBONGENI. Ready . . . target centre below . . . release depth charges . . . bombs . . . torpedoes . . . go!

They watch. The bombs fall. A moment of silence and then a terrible explosion. They separate, come together detonating each other. Light reduces to stark overhead shaft.

BOTH. Momeeeee! Aunti-i-i-eee! He-e-e-l-l-p!

Blackout.

Scene Twenty-five

South African television news theme is proclaimed in darkness.

MBONGENI. News!

Lights on.

PERCY (*in pink nose, proudly holds a cardboard TV screen shape around his face*): Good evening. The United Nations Security Council is still waiting further information on the explosion which completely destroyed Capetown and its famous Table Mountain. (*Bland smile.*) United Nations nuclear sensors have recorded distinct signs of nuclear disturbance in the Southern African sector. Investigators have suggested a strong possibility of a mishap to a SAA Military Helicopter carrying a nuclear missile over the bay. However, Mrs Fatima Mossop, domestic servant, Sea Point, a freak survivor of the calamity, insisted that the explosion emanated from a human figure walking across the bay from the Island, supporting the superstition that the nuclear-type explosion was an inevitable result of a bomb attack on Morena. The Prime Minister himself continues to deny any relationship between Morena and the agitator imprisoned

'Good evening.'

on the Island. Mrs Fatima Mossop is still under observation by the state psychiatrists. Well, that is all for tonight. Goodnight. (*Fade on fixed smile.*)

Scene Twenty-six

The graveyard. Mbongeni in a hat and dust-coat is weeding and singing Zuluboy's song from Scene Eighteen. Percy is sleeping on the boxes. Mbongeni sees him, rouses him.

MBONGENI. Hey! Hey! Hey! This is not a park bench. It's a tombstone. This is a cemetery, it's not Joubert Park.

PERCY (*groggy*): I'm sorry, I should know better.

MBONGENI. You want Joubert Park? You want Joubert Park? You catch the number fifty-four bus. Or you want Zola Park? You catch a Zola taxi. Or you want to have a look at the ducks? Go to the Zoo Läke. But don't sit on my tombstones. Please.

PERCY. Okay, I'm sorry about that. Can I have a look around?

MBONGENI. Oh, well if you want to have a look around, look around, but don't sit around! The dead are having a hard enough time. These tombstones are bladdy heavy!

PERCY. Aaahh, tell me, do you keep your tombstones in alphabetical order?

MBONGENI. Yeah. What do you want?

PERCY. Where's 'L'?

MBONGENI. You want 'L'?

PERCY. Ja.

MBONGENI. Serious? Okay. Right there. That whole line is 'L'. By that big tombstone. See? Livingstone . . . Lamele . . . Lusiti . . . Lizi . . .

PERCY. Have you got any Lazarus here?

MBONGENI. Lazarus? Lazarus? Oh, Israel Lazarus! That was a very good man! You mean that one? American Half-Price Dealers? That was a very good man, I used to work for him in 1962. But he's not dead yet! Why are you looking for his grave here?

Morena arises.

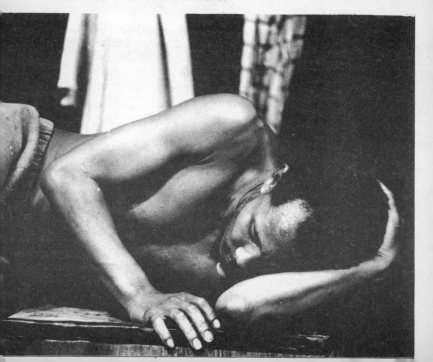

PERCY. I'm just looking for something to do.

MBONGENI. But this face I know. Are you his son?

PERCY. No, not his.

MBONGENI. Then who are you?

PERCY. Morena.

MBONGENI. You? Morena? Aaay suka! They killed him. That is his tombstone.

PERCY. Oh no, Baba. Have you forgotten? I will always come back after three days, bombs or no bombs.

MBONGENI. Hay! Morena! Aawu nkulunkulu wami! [Oh my God!]

PERCY. Ssssshhhh! Please, don't shout my name.

MBONGENI. Do you remember me?

PERCY. Who are you?

MBONGENI. Zuluboy from Coronation Brickyard!

PERCY. Hey! Zuluboy! (*They embrace.*) What are you doing here?

MBONGENI. I'm working here at the cemetery. I'm disguised from the police! Lazarus . . . Lazarus . . . aaaahhh! Now I understand! Morena, you're looking for people to raise!

PERCY. Ja!

MBONGENI. But why didn't you ask me?

PERCY. How would I know?

MBONGENI. I know exactly who my people want! Come, let us look at these tombstones.

Mbongeni leads Percy in a dance around the cemetery, singing

Mbongeni stops, Percy beside him. He points to a corner of the audience.

MBONGENI. Morena! Here's our 'L' — ALBERT LUTHULI — the Father of our Nation! Raise him Morena!

PERCY. Woza Albert! [Rise up Albert!]

Mbongeni falls over, stunned then ecstatic.

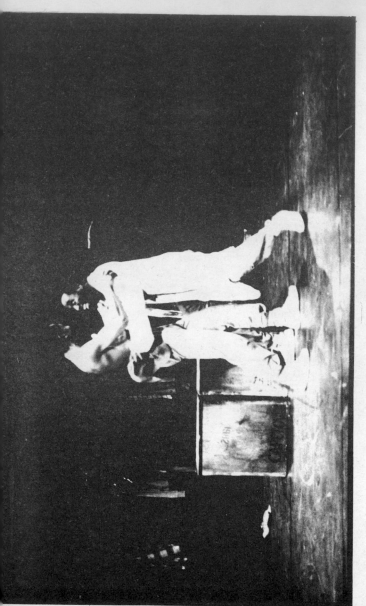

Zuluboy and Morena.

'They dance around the cemetery.'

BOTH (*singing*):
    Yamemeza inkosi yethu
    Yathi ma thambo hlanganani
    Oyawa vusa amaqhawe amnyama
    Wathi kuwo

    [Our Lord is calling.
    He's calling for the bones of the dead to join together.
    He's raising up the black heroes.
    He calls to them

MBONGENI (*addressing the risen but invisible Albert Luthuli*):
    Hey, Luthuli uyangibona mina? U Zulu boy. Ngakhula phansi
    kwakho e-Stanger. [Hey, Luthuli, do you remember me? I'm
    Zulu boy. I grew up in Stanger.]

They dance on, repeating the song.

BOTH (*singing*):
    Yamemeza inkosi yethu
    Yathi ma thambo hlanganani
    Oyawa vusa amaqhawe amnyama
    Wathi kuwo

    [Our Lord is calling.
    He's calling for the bones of the dead to join together.
    He's raising up the black heroes.
    He calls to them

Mbongeni stops, Percy beside him.

MBONGENI. Morena! Robert Sobukwe! He taught us Black
    Power! Raise him!

PERCY. Woza Robert!

MBONGENI (*ecstatic*): Hau Manaliso! Manaliso!

They dance on.

BOTH (*singing*):
    Yamemezo inkosi yethu
    Yathi ma thambo hlanganani
    Oyawa vusa amaqhawe amnyama
    Wathi kuwo

    [Our Lord is calling.
    He's calling for the bones of the dead to join together.
    He's raising up the black heroes.
    He calls to them

'Woza Steve!'

'WOZA ALBERT!'

MBONGENI. Lilian Ngoyi! She taught our mothers about freedom. Raise her!

PERCY. Woza Lilian!

MBONGENI (*spins with joy*): Woza Lilian! — Hey Lilian, uya mbona uMorena? Uvuswe uMorena. [Come Lilian — hey Lilian, do you see Morena? It's Morena who raised you.]

They dance on.

BOTH (*singing*):
Yamemeza inkosi yethu
Hathi ma thambo hlanganani
Oyawa vusa amaqhawe amnyama
Wathi kuwo

[Our Lord is calling.
He's calling for the bones of the dead to join together.
He's raising up the black heroes.
He calls to them

MBONGENI. Steve Biko! The hero of our children! Please Morena — Please raise him!

PERCY. Woza Steve!

MBONGENI. Steve! Steve! Uyangikhumbula ngikulandela e Kingwilliams-town? [Steve, do you remember me, following you in Kingswilliamstown?]

BOTH (*dancing*): Woza Bram Fischer! . . . Woza Ruth First! . . . Woza Griffith Mxenge . . . Woza Hector Peterson . . . (*They stop, arms raised triumphantly.*) WOZA ALBERT!!!

Blackout.

GLOSSARY

Words

baas, basie — subservient words for boss

baba — father, a term of respect

bra — brother

hostel — all male housing compound serving the mines and industrial areas

kaffir — nigger

Morena — Sir, or Lord, term of respect

Passbook — Every black man and woman over the age of sixteen is forced by law to carry at all times, a passbook, also known as a dompass. It contains information about birth, family, background, employment taxation etc. If at any time the police discover a person without a passbook, immediate arrest follows. The passbook is a major symbol of oppression in South Africa.

rand — South African unit of currency, one dollar

woza — rise up

Places

Albert Street — This Johannesburg street is the location of the Pass Office that controls the influx of black workers to and from the city. Workers often line up for days awaiting permits to seek work. A black born outside the city becomes an illegal immigrant if he loses his job and can be 'endorsed' out of the city back to a homeland. Black men, legal or otherwise, wait in Albert Street for whites driving by who are looking for labourers.

Homelands — Also known as 'Bantustans' and 'Reserves', the homelands are the tribal areas set aside for blacks. They are run by governments set up by the South African regime. Rather than being 'homes', they are areas of great devastation and poverty that offer few opportunities for employment. Because young men are recruited away by white industries and mines, homelands such as Kwazulu, the Transkei and Bophutatswana are populated largely by women, children and old people. Blacks employed in white areas may not bring their families with them. Consequently they often live in all-male hostels, and are able to see their families for only a few weeks at Christmas. Through the apartheid policy of homelands, only 13% of all South African territory is ceded to more than 20 million blacks. The rest of the land, which includes the richest agricultural and mineral areas, is reserved for five million whites.

Robben Island — Surrounded by the icy Atlantic Ocean off Cape Town, Robben Island is the high security prison where black political prisoners are confined.

Soweto — This huge black ghetto outside Johannesburg was the scene of the Childrens' Uprising in 1976, which began as a protest against poor education, became a protest against all government policies and ended in riots and the massacre of at least 467 people.

Sun City — A huge pleasure resort and gambling casino in the heart of Bophutatswana. Here top entertainers like Frank Sinatra, Liza Minelli, Olivia Newton-John, Ann-Margaret perform for enormous fees. Here gambling, bare-breasted dancers, miscegenation — all illegal in South Africa — are permitted to South Africans. Sun City offers employment, but it is surrounded by terrible poverty.

People

Albert Luthuli — Born in 1898, Albert Luthuli was a Zulu chief instrumental in organizing the 1952 Defiance Campaign — a civil rights crusade in which thousands of blacks demonstrated against apartheid. The same year, Luthuli became president-general of the African National Congress. Arrested in 1956, he was released after a year, but in 1959 was banished to his small farm under the Suppression of Communism Act, which prohibited him from attending meetings, from writing for publication, and from being quoted. He was awarded the Nobel Peace Prize in 1960, published abroad his autobiography, *Let My People Go*, in 1962, and died in 1967.

Robert Sobukwe — Born in 1924, Robert Sobukwe was a militant college leader and one of the founders of the Pan Africanist Congress. He was elected its president in 1959. One of the leaders of the 1960 anti-pass laws protests, he was arrested and charged with inciting the destruction of pass books. After being sentenced to three years imprisonment, Sobukwe was released in 1963 but promptly detained through an act of parliament for an additional six years on Robben Island. This so-called "Sobukwe clause" permits indefinite detention of political prisoners after their sentences have been served. Finally released in 1969, Sobukwe was restricted by bans and confined to the Kimberley district until his death in 1978.

Bram Fischer — Born into a prominent Afrikaner family in 1908, Bram Fischer was the son of a Judge President of the Orange Free State and grandson of a Prime Minister of the Orange River Colony. He became radicalized as a law student at Oxford. After becoming a lawyer, he led the defence in a number of political trials, including the Treason Trial of 1956-1960 and the Rivonia Trial of 1963-1964. In September 1964, he was arrested and charged under the Suppression of Communism Act, but fled underground to continue his political activism. Re-arrested within a year, he was sentenced to life imprisonment, and died in 1975.

Lilian Ngoyi — Within one year of joining the Women's League of the African National Congress in 1952, Lilian Ngoyi became its president. Her eloquence as a public speaker and energy as an organizer made her a target of the government. In 1956 she was arrested and became one of those prosecuted in the massive Treason Trial that did not end until 1960. Restricted for many years by various bans and forms of house arrest that confined her to her home and prohibited her from having visitors and from holding a job, she died in 1980.

Steve Biko — Born in 1946, Steve Biko became the first president of the All-Black South African Students' Organization in 1968. It and the Black Peoples' Convention, which Biko also helped form, were at the forefront of articulating the emerging philosophy of black consciousness. He was served with a five-year banning order in 1973. In 1975 he was arrested and held for 137 days without charge or trial. Following the Soweto riots of 1976, he was arrested and held in solitary confinement for 101 days. In 1977 he was again arrested and twenty-seven days later became the twentieth person to die in police custody over an eighteen month period. Despite numerous arrests, Biko was never convicted of a single crime.

Ruth First — Author and teacher.
Born into a politically radical family in Johannesburg, she studied social science. From the mid-forties she worked with

African mine strikers, and with Nelson Mandela and others of
the African National Congress. She was Johannesburg editor of
radical journals which were successively banned, and acting
secretary of the Communist Party. Among the 156 accused and
later acquitted in the Treason Trial in 1956, she was then
banned and house arrested. In 1963 she was held in solitary
confinement for 117 days. A leading member of the A.N.C.,
while running a university department in Mozambique she
was killed by a letter bomb on August 17 1982.

David Rudkin	*The Saxon Shore*
	The Sons of Light
	The Triumph of Death
Willy Russell	*Educating Rita, Stags & Hens* and *Blood Brothers*
	Shirley Valentine and *One for the Road*
Jean-Paul Sartre	*Crime Passionnel*
Ntozake Shange	*for colored girls who have considered suicide/when the rainbow is enuf* & *Spell #7*
Sam Shepard	*A Lie of the Mind*
Wole Soyinka	*Madmen and Specialists*
	The Jero Plays
	Death and the King's Horseman
	A Play of Giants
C.P. Taylor	*And a Nightingale Sang . . .*
	Good
Yuri Trifonov	*Exchange*
Peter Whelan	*The Accrington Pals*
Nigel Williams	*Line 'Em*
	Class Enemy
Victoria Wood	*Good Fun* and *Talent*
Theatre Workshop	*Oh What a Lovely War*